ANY C

by

Bil Keane

FAWCETT GOLD MEDAL • NEW YORK

ANY CHILDREN?

Published by special arrangement with The Register & Tribune
Syndicate, Inc. by Fawcett Gold Medal Books, a unit of CBS
Publications, the Consumer Publishing Division of CBS Inc.

ISBN: 0-449-14116-0

Printed in the United States of America

10 9 8 7 6 5

"Does anybody want an egg? I have one open."

"I can't wait till we get biology 'cause I wanna learn all about dead frogs."

"I wanted the BLUE cup."

"Want me to go get Mommy to kiss it?"

"When you blow through here it turns your breath into music."

"The Tippits call their mother 'Ma,' the Turners say
'Mother' and we call you 'Mommy.' Which
one's right?"

"Daddy! Do UFO's have blinking red lights?"

"I can't open it — it's locked!"

"Don't scrape your feet on the carpet before you kiss
Daddy or you'll get a shock!"

"Bless Mommy twice and Daddy twice and . . ."

"I forgot to say my prayers last night."

"Grandma only put three hugs and kisses on my card, and she gave PJ six."

"Wow! Look! ANTS!"

"My shoes aren't muddy any more. I walked through a puddle."

"Jeffy, if you don't stop watchin' we'll NEVER get any birds to move in."

"If the Easter bunny gets sick, does Santa come instead?"

"Do one HOT PINK, then an AVOCADO one, then HARVEST GOLD, and . . ."

"What's God gonna do with all that money?"

"Mrs. Bombeck said we look JUST PRECIOUS!"

"Mommy, this cup and saucer don't rhyme."

"Look, Mommy! I found a little hunch worm!"

"Next can we stop at a hamburger station?"

"Remember? Daddy said for me to try and stay off my sore heel."

"You missed a spot, Mommy."

"I won't be able to do my 'rithmetic homework tonight. Your calculator has a dead battery."

"Guess what, Mommy — you were right! My teacher
says milk is good for us."

"Can I wear long pants to play in so you won't have to scrub my knees?"

"But, how do you KNOW there's no practice today?"

"Wait till Mommy's finished. She can't hear with her ears full."

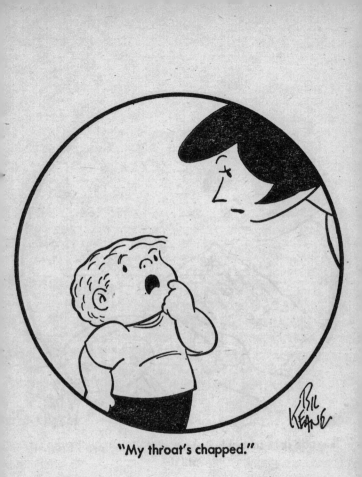

"My throat's chapped."

"I made it in school but the bell rang before I finished it."

"You needn't hide. It's nobody you have to kiss."

"How's your after shave lotion, Daddy — almost gone?"

"If the bees make honey, do butterflies make butter?"

"Some weeds try to fool you by having flowers."

"This is the king, and this is the queen, and this is the prince. His name is Jack."

"See? Every time I pull one out another one pops up!"

"Next time just push ONE floor, not ALL of them!"

"The moon is up there somewhere, but I guess they've got their lights out."

"Summer's here! Daddy's gonna lawn the grass!"

"How long before the flowers will be born?"

"Seat belts might keep you safe, but they don't let you see much."

."We're not runnin' through the house, Daddy —
we're JOGGIN'!"

"Billy left this out and the water is all loose again."

"Look, Mommy! The birds are havin' a meeting!"

"I don't know that priest's last name, but his first name is Father."

"Hurry with the jar, Mommy! The lightning bugs are TICKLIN' me!"

"Why do they put the peanuts in these little pack-
ages?"

"Y'know, I've been little as long as I can remember."

"Jason's mom was really SURPRISED when I came to stay all night. Jason forgot to tell her."

"Row, row, row your boat — gently down the stream
— Marilyn, Marilyn, Marilyn, Marilyn . . ."

"Mommy, does Goldilocks belong in 'The Three Pigs' or 'The Three Bears'?"

"I wish we had a bigger indoors."

"But we can't go on vacation next week! That's the week Mrs. Lincicome is payin' me $2 to feed her cat!"

"Billy, tell me if my turn signals are on."

"Yes . . . no . . . yes . . . no . . . yes . . ."

"Don't worry, we're not movin'! We're going on vacation!"

"Before we leave let's see if we have all the necessities — road maps, credit cards, emergency lollipops . . ."

"Now hear this! The first one who says 'How much further is it, Daddy?' gets out and walks!"

"GREEN LIGHT!"

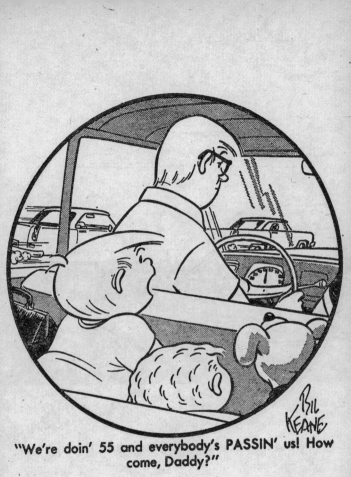

"We're doin' 55 and everybody's PASSIN' us! How come, Daddy?"

"What time does the next deer cross, Daddy?"

"Can't you wait till we get to the next gas station?"

"THERE'S a good place, Daddy! Let's stop for hamburgers!"

"We're making good time . . . OOPS! What was THAT?"

"Why did you pack the tire underneath all this other stuff, Daddy?"

"Oh, boy! This is the best part of the trip so far!"

"Daddy didn't wash up after he changed the tire."

"Hi, Grandma! We're here! Wanna play cards with me?"

"I've gotten too BIG for you to pick up — right, Granddad?"

" . . . And Kittycat likes only DRY cat food, and Jeffy
doesn't eat peas, and Daddy stays away
from desserts, and . . ."

"Boy! Grandma's TV screen is TINY!"

"PJ sits in Mommy's old high chair, Billy sits on the
phone book, Jeffy gets the stool and I sit
on the cushion — right, Grandma?"

"Grandma, I can't find your bathroom."

"But, where's the LAST one I sent you, Grandma?"

"It IS SO a Grandfather's clock! It's Granddad's, isn't it?"

"Why don't you have any. things on these bottom shelves, Grandma?"

"Granddad, 'bout what time does your ice cream man usually get here?"

"If you find any toys we left behind, Grandma, that's okay — you can play with them."

" 'Bye, Grandma! 'Bye, Granddad! Don't cry — we'll
be back to visit some other time!"

"Maybe that police car wants to pass, Daddy — he's
followin' right behind us with his red
lights flashing!"

"He's supposed to read you your rights, Daddy."

"Sorry to stop you, sir, but I thought you'd like to
know we caught the reckless driver who ran
you off the road a few miles back."

"Stop the car, Daddy — I feel sick!"

"We're gettin' close to home 'cause there's our gas
station and there's A.J.'s Market and that's
Potter's tennis court and . . ."

"Oh, boy! Home again and NOTHIN' TO DO!"

"Daddy, I think you forgot to kiss me goodnight."

"Don't wash my mug any more, Mommy. My name is startin' to come off."

"... strawberry, maple nut, chocolate ribbon, daiquiri ice, lemon sherbet, raspberry sherbet, and grape ice."

"What are they again, Daddy?"

"That's all right for lollipops, but you have to hold pencils a different way."

"It's a salesman, I think. Should I tell him we don't want any?"

"We're squirrels, lady. Got any peanuts?"

"This cut is from fallin' off my skates and this one's
from Ferrell's fence and . . ."
"Yeah, well, I got this bump playin' baseball and this is
from chasin' Barfy and . . ."

"Let Dolly alone — tend to your own knitting."

"We're not knitting. We're coloring!"

"How come they never have presidents in fairy tales?"

"Don't get it too close to the sun!"

"Excuse me, gentlemen, I said I'd wave bye-bye."

"In case you don't know what color this is, it's sharp-truce."

"Look what PJ can do, Mommy! It's his imitation of Kittycat!"

"Know why this show is in black and white? They couldn't find their crayons."

"If a lamb followed ME to school, I'd use him for Show and Tell."

"I knew you were comin' to visit 'cause we got out the picture you gave us and hung it up."

"Look, the moon is turned on all the way!"

"No, this is a badminton racket. Tennis rackets have bigger windows."

"Mommy! Daddy's gettin' something out of the food-gerator!"

"Cream of mushroom soup?"   "Yuk."
"Chicken croquettes?"   "Yuk."
"Spanish omelette?"   "Yuk."
"Pie and ice cream?"   "Yum."

"Mommy, how many sneezes am I allowed before
Jeffy can stop God-blessing me?"

"'Gallons' is old-fashioned, Daddy. You should ask for 42.3 liters."

"Valerie Watson's daddy is pushing her on the swings!"

"Hey! That's pretty good — for a mommy!"

"Is it okay to use your sky, Mrs. Morgan?"

"When Daddy stirs the water with those, it makes the boat go."

"Hi, Mommy! We're medicating!"

"'G' is like a 'C' with a little shelf on it."

"Our daddy's coat is the one that's fallin' apart inside."

"Mommy! The door's knockin'!"

"Daddy, TALK the words so I can hear 'em."

"Don't you like Mike's freckles? Can I grow some, too?"

"The chair put its foot out and tripped me!"

"I wanted it on the rocks."

"Somebodys ate two candy bars last night!"

"When did God have his picture taken?"

"Do doctors ever get sick like real people?"

"Grandma sent us new wallets! Can we have something to fill 'em up?"

"When I say my prayers my fingers hug each other."

"Wow! Is that man gonna have a baby?"

Have Fun with the Family Circus

☑	ANY CHILDREN?	14116	$1.50
☑	DADDY'S LITTLE HELPERS	14384	$1.50
☑	DOLLY HIT ME BACK!	14273	$1.50
☑	GOOD MORNING SUNSHINE!	14356	$1.50
☐	FOR THIS I WENT TO COLLEGE?	14069	$1.50
☑	NOT ME!	14333	$1.50
☐	I'M TAKING A NAP	14144	$1.50
☐	LOOK WHO'S HERE	14207	$1.50
☐	PEACE, MOMMY, PEACE	14145	$1.50
☐	PEEKABOO! I LOVE YOU!	14174	$1.50
☑	WANNA BE SMILED AT?	14118	$1.50
☑	WHEN'S LATER, DADDY?	14124	$1.50
☑	MINE	14056	$1.50
☑	SMILE!	14172	$1.50
☐	JEFFY'S LOOKIN' AT ME!	14096	$1.50
☑	CAN I HAVE A COOKIE?	14155	$1.50
☑	THE FAMILY CIRCUS	14068	$1.50
☐	HELLO, GRANDMA?	14169	$1.50
☑	I NEED A HUG	14147	$1.50
☑	QUIET! MOMMY'S ASLEEP!	13930	$1.50

where's PJ
I can't untie my shoes

Buy them at your local bookstore or use this handy coupon for ordering.